Valentina's Fun Day Out

By

Belinda Booth

ShieldCrest

ISBN: 978-1-913839-49-9

A CIP catalogue record for this book
is available from the British Library

MMXXIII

Published by
ShieldCrest Publishing.,
The Hawthorns, Cemetery Road
Boston, Lincs, PE20 3BT
Tel: +44 (0) 333 8000 890
www.shieldcrest.co.uk

Firstly, I'd like to thank my husband, John, for his ongoing support.

To my six beautiful grandchildren, Lleyton, Josh, Elliot, Valentina and twins Kobe and Emilia. I love you all.

I would also like to say a big thank you to my Mum.
I wouldn't be the person I am today if it wasn't for her.

It was a beautiful, sunny morning. Valentina was getting ready to go out with Nanny and Grandad. She sat at the table eating her breakfast.

"Valentina," Mum said, "you need to finish your cereal. Nanny and Grandad will be here soon."

"I don't like cereal," she said, pushing the bowl away. "I want to go out *now*."

"You need to have your breakfast first, before you can go out," said Mum. "Would you like a bowl of fruit instead?"

Valentina crossed her arms and scrunched her face. "I'm not hungry," she said. "I don't like fruits. Fruits are for babies."

"Oh dear," Mum said, "someone's grumpy this morning."

Mum walked over to the kitchen to get Valentina a bowl of fruit.

"You *are* a baby," said her brother, Josh, who was sitting next to her.

"I'm not a baby," she said. "I'm four." Valentina shouted to her mum. "Mummy, Josh called me a cry baby."

"I didn't," said Josh, laughing.

Valentina got off her chair and went under the table. She wasn't happy.

Mum came back with a bowl of fruit. "Oh, where is Valentina?" Mum said, jokingly. "Has anybody seen her?"

Valentina quickly popped her head out from under the table. "Mummy, I'm here. Look, I'm here," she said, giggling.

Mum handed her the bowl of fruit.

"Thank you, Mummy," she said. Then she went back under the table and ate all her fruit.

"I've finished eating," she shouted from under the table, with the empty bowl in her hand. "Thank you, Mummy."

The doorbell rang. Valentina ran to the door. Mum followed behind her and opened the door.

"Hello, Nanny. Hello, Grandad," Mum said.

"Are you ready to go out?" Grandad asked Valentina.

"Yes, I'm ready," she said with a big smile. She ran to get her kitty backpack.

She came back to the door. Nanny held her hand and off they went.

Mum waved. "See you later, Valentina. Have a good day."

"Bye, Mummy," said Valentina. "See you later."

They all walked towards the car. Valentina was really excited.

"Would you like to go to the shops?" said Nanny. Valentina nodded her head, with another big smile on her face.

Grandad drove to a big shopping centre called Crystal Peaks. Valentina had been there before with Mum.

Grandad parked the car outside Dog and Gate. Dog and Gate was a big shop which sold children's toys, children's clothes, and dog and cat toys. It also had a big ice cream parlour in the middle of the shop.

Dog and Gate was very popular with children because animals were allowed in, so children were allowed to shop with their dogs. There were dog stations all over the shop just in case the dogs got hungry and needed food and water.

"Look!" said Valentina as they walked into the shop.

There was a boy standing with his little dog. Valentina ran to the dog, but before she could ask the boy if she could stroke it, the little dog jumped on her.

"Hello, doggy," Valentina said as the dog tried to lick her face. She broke into a fit of giggles and couldn't stop laughing. "No doggy, no," she said, as she bent down to stroke it. "Can I have a dog?" she said, stroking the dog gently.

"Not today," laughed Grandad.

"Come on then," said Nanny. "Let's go and do some shopping."

Valentina stood up and waved goodbye to the dog. "Bye doggy," she said. The little dog wagged its tail and the boy smiled and waved back to Valentina.

Valentina's eyes lit up. There were different things to look at – sparkly dresses, toys and books.

She spotted some sparkly dresses. There was a pink one and a blue one that she really liked. She held up both dresses. "I like them both," she said. "Please can I have them?"

"Of course, you can have them," said Grandad. "Put them in the trolley."

"Thank you, Grandad," she said as she quickly put the dresses in the trolley.

Next, they all walked down the book aisle which had all kinds of books – dog books, cat books, helicopter books. She went past a mermaid book.

"Valentina," said Grandad. "Do you like mermaids?"

"Yes, I do," she said. But then she spotted a *Scruff the Dog* book. "Look," she said, pointing at the book. "It's a *Scruff the Dog* book". She could hardly speak with excitement and stood on her tiptoes to get the book off the shelf. She looked at the book. "*Scruff the Dog*," she said as she turned the pages."

"That's your favourite book," said Nanny. Valentina smiled and nodded her head. "Put it in the trolley," said Nanny.

"Thank you," said Valentina.

"Should we get some ice cream?" said Grandad.

"Yes please," she said.

They headed to the ice cream parlour. It was in the middle of the shop.

"Ice cream is my favourite," she said.

SCRUFF
the dog

LOVE

emily

BOOKS

There were lots of children sitting down and eating their ice creams. The chairs and tables were all painted in bright colours and the chairs were shaped like dogs and cats.

Valentina ran to the counter and pressed her nose against the glass to look at the ice creams.

There were all different kinds of ice creams – strawberry, chocolate, raspberry and vanilla. Valentina didn't know which flavour to choose.

"What flavour would you like?" said the lady behind the counter.

"Mmm," she said. "I would like a strawberry cone and a chocolate cone please."

"You can only have one," said Nanny.

"I want two! Why can't I have two? I want strawberry and chocolate," she said and then burst into tears.

"Oh, Valentina," said Nanny. "Don't cry."

"Come here," said Nanny, and she gave Valentina a big cuddle.

"Please don't cry," said the lady behind the counter. "I'll see what I can do. Would you like me to put a scoop of chocolate and strawberry on your cone?"

"Yes please," said Valentina, wiping her tears. The lady handed her the ice cream.

"What do you say to the kind lady," said Grandad.
"Thank you," she said. The lady smiled. Nanny ordered a strawberry ice cream and Grandad ordered a chocolate ice cream.

Valentina went to sit down with nanny and grandad, she sat on a dog shaped chair. "Mmm," she said, licking her ice cream. "This ice cream is yummy."

When she had finished her ice cream, Grandad said, "Come on, let's get you home."

They all left the shop and Grandad drove to Valentina's house. Mum was at the door waiting and Valentina ran to Mum.

"Did you have a nice day?" said Mum.

"Yes, I did," said Valentina. She got all the shopping from the bag and showed Mum.

"You've been spoilt," said Mum.

"Can I go out shopping again tomorrow?" Valentina said, jumping up and down.

They all laughed. "We'll see," said Nanny.

Nanny and Grandad said goodbye to Valentina and Mum.

"Goodbye, Nanny. Goodbye, Grandad, thank you for taking me out." She waved as Mum shut the door.

About the Author

Originally from Zimbabwe, Africa, Belinda has four Children, Clayton, Bonolo, Charlene and Ashton and six grandchildren to whom this book is dedicated. She now lives in Sheffield and is married to John.

Belinda is an animal lover and wrote her first book when living in Botswana. Her granddaughter, Valentina, inspired her to write this book after she and her husband took her shopping. They had so much fun that she decided to capture the moment.

"Valentina's Fun Day Out" is the first in a series, all of which will be packed with fun and adventure. Look out for "Valentina Gets a Dog" which will be out soon. All the characters in her books are real people, Valentina, Josh, Elliot grandchildren, Nanny me, Grandad my husband and Mum, our daughter Charlene.

www.ingramcontent.com/pod-product-compliance
Lightning Source LLC
Chambersburg PA
CBHW040849100426

* 9 7 8 1 9 1 3 8 3 9 4 9 9 *